CONTENTS

INTRODUCTION

In the world of corporate training, the pursuit of engagement and learning is a constant challenge. As trainers, we understand the delicate balance between imparting knowledge and ensuring that participants remain actively involved in the learning process.

Enter "Purposeful Play: 99 Interactive Training Activities." This book is a curated collection of 99 icebreakers, energizers, games, and exercises designed to infuse a sense of purpose and liveliness into your training sessions. Drawing from the author's experiences, these activities have been chosen for their potential to create genuine connections, spark meaningful discussions, and facilitate skill development. Whether you want to make learning more exciting for your participants or add new activities to your toolkit, this book is your guide to making training better through experiential learning.

Each activity is crafted with a specific intention – whether it's to break down barriers between participants, re-energize a group after a long session, promote teamwork, or foster creativity. They are tools meant to empower you to facilitate engaging and effective learning experiences. Whether you're a novice or an experienced trainer, there's something valuable for everyone in this book.

Remember that purposeful play is a means to an end – not the end itself. As you explore the activities within these pages, keep your participants' growth and development at the forefront of your mind. Approach each activity with an open heart and a willingness to adapt. View them as tools that, when combined with your expertise and intuition, can elevate your training sessions.

The true magic happens when the activities align with your training objectives and the unique dynamics of your group. May this book inspire you to inject a sense of curiosity, camaraderie, and connection into your training sessions, one purposeful play at a time.

PURPOSEFUL PLAY

1. *the process of intentionally planning, designing and facilitating activities with the specific intention of enhancing the learning experience.*

2. *it incorporates elements of playfulness, creativity, and engagement.*

BENEFITS OF USING TRAINING ACTIVITIES

Training activities offer a range of advantages that enrich the learning experience and improve learning outcomes, including:

Engagement

Activities are inherently fun and enjoyable, which can motivate individuals to actively participate in the training process. When learners are engaged, they are more likely to pay attention, retain information, and apply what they have learned.

Active learning

Training activities promote active learning, allowing participants to apply their knowledge and skills in a practical context. Instead of passively absorbing information, participants actively participate in the activities, make decisions, solve problems, and experience the consequences of their actions. This hands-on approach enhances understanding and retention of the material.

Social interaction

Many training activities promote dialogue and discussions amongst the learners, which encourage them to talk to each other, creating common bonds and making them more comfortable with each other. This social element facilitates team building and creates a conducive environment for learners to be their authentic selves.

Collaborative learning

Training activities typically offer opportunities for collaborative learning, allowing learners to work together, communicate, and solve problems as a team. Collaboration promotes knowledge sharing and encourages learners to consider different perspectives. This collaborative element enhances the overall learning experience.

Knowledge retention
Training activities create memorable experiences that increase knowledge retention. When information is presented in a fun and interactive way, it is more likely to stick in the participants' minds, increasing the likelihood of them applying what they have learned in real-life scenarios.

Overall, training activities offer a valuable complement to traditional training methods, making learning more enjoyable and effective. While they offer numerous benefits, they are most effective when used as part of a well-rounded approach to training and design with clear objectives in mind.

PIES APPROACH

Creating and leading a meaningful activity experience is not a complex task, but it does require careful consideration. To ensure that you're heading in the right direction in developing an engaging and effective training session, keep in mind PIES (Purposeful, Inclusive, Easy to Understand, and Safety) when planning and facilitating the activities.

Purposeful

Clearly define the purpose of the activity and what you aim to achieve through it. Ask yourself if the activities can meaningfully contribute to one or more of these goals - energize the group, promote social interaction, and/or reinforce learning. When conducting the games, guide the participants purposefully towards the desired outcome, offering questions and hints as needed, while allowing them to maintain control of their experience.

Inclusive

Create a supportive atmosphere that encourages active participation from everyone. Design the activity to cater to the needs of different individuals and ensure that everyone gets an equal opportunity to lead, participate, and showcase their skills during the activities. Encourage quieter participants to share their ideas and make sure no one dominates the activities.

Easy to understand

Keep the activities simple and the instructions clear. Participants should be able to quickly grasp and engage in the activities without lengthy or complicated explanations. To improve understanding, use visual aids and demonstrate the instructions when explaining them.

Safe

Create a safe environment for the activities, both physically and psychologically. Choose a suitable space for the activity and provide the group with a briefing on safety rules and potential hazards before commencing. Participants should feel psychologically secure to voice their thoughts, take risks, and express their ideas, as these are essential elements for effective teamwork. Avoid putting them in humiliating or embarrassing situations, such as pressuring them to do something in front of the group when they are clearly uncomfortable.

ACTIVITY FACILITATION TIPS

For purposeful play to be effective, tweak how you organize and conduct the activities to match the training goals and the group's characteristics. Here are some facilitation tips to help you make the most of the training activities:

1. **Encourage competition**

   Competition generates excitement, which in turn motivates active participation. Here are some ways to incorporate competition:
   - Against others: Divide participants into multiple teams.
   - Against targets: Set goals for groups to achieve.
   - Against themselves: Challenge teams to improve their previous records.

2. **Assign roles**

   To ensure everyone contributes, assign various roles to participants. This will lessen the bystander effect and reduce the influence of dominant participants.

3. **Ensure equal participation**

   To ensure active involvement, stipulate that every team member must take equal turns performing tasks, rather than relying solely on more capable members. For activities requiring restarts due to rule violations, make it mandatory to rearrange the order of members to avoid the same individuals always initiating the activity.

4. **Allow room for brainstorming**

   Providing minimal or vague instructions encourages more team discussion and creativity.

5. **Combine planning and task execution time**
   Not assigning a fixed or dedicated planning time allows you to observe how teams manage time – do they dive straight into action or take time to strategize?

6. **Infusing change**
   Injecting changes energizers the group and increases the challenge. Changes can involve reshuffling teams, adding new requirements, or removing resources. Be cautious about altering rules during the activity, as this can frustrate adult learners. If changing rules align with the desired outcome, present the change in a way that relates to the participants. For instance, say "new regulations have been introduced by the authorities."

7. **Implement rewards and penalties**
   Employ rewards and penalties when appropriate to motivate participation. Rewards need not be material; they can be intangible, like an extra 5-minute break. Penalties might involve packing logistics or setting up the next activity. Another penalty option is performing a song and dance, but ensure participants are comfortable with this kind of spotlight.

8. **Review learning before or during the activity**
   Typically, debriefs for activities occur after the experience concludes. However, reviewing the learning before the activity starts and while it's happening can enhance the learning process. Here's how:
   - Before: Talk about the learning subject with the group and then challenge them to put it into practice during the activity.

- During: After completing one round of the activity, guide a review session and instruct them to apply the insights gained to the next round.

9. **Frame the activity**

Present the activity as a real task to enhance the transfer of learning to the workplace. For example, portray the group as a team of consultants solving a client's problem. The activity's resources could represent the budget, and the activity duration mirrors the project deadline.

10. **Flip chart recording**

Observe participants in action to identify relevant behaviors and interactions for training, then jot them down on a flip chart or writing board and lead a discussion around these observations.

ACTIVITY DEBRIEFING QUESTIONS

People are more likely to remember and internalize what they've learned when they take the time to reflect on their experiences. Here's a list of questions that can help participants reflect on their experiences during the activity:

1. Why did you succeed (or not)?

2. How did your team collaborate?

3. What obstacles did you face and how did you overcome them?

4. If you were to redo the activity, what would you change?

5. How did you generate ideas to solve the problem?

6. Can you provide specific instances of collaborative behaviors in this activity?

7. What behaviors were effective/ineffective in completing the task?

8. Can you give specific examples of effective communication during the exercise?

9. What did a fellow team member do that was really helpful?

10. Who took on leadership roles during the activity and what were their actions?

11. How did the group identify the problem that needed solving?

12. How did the team handle disagreements?

13. How were group decisions made?

14. What did you learn from this activity?

15. What lessons can you apply back to your work?

ACTIVITY CLASSIFICATION

Many training activities can fulfill various learning objectives and serve different purposes. However, to make navigation easier, the activities in this book are categorized into the following seven main themes that align with their primary uses and outcomes:

1. **Icebreakers**
    Activities that help people get to know each other, fostering a relaxed atmosphere. They can also deepen connections among those already acquainted.

2. **Energizers**
    Quick and fun activities that boost energy and excitement in a group. They can be used anytime to increase alertness and refocus participants during training.

3. **Training introduction**
    Fun exercises to arouse participants' interest in the training and help them explore new subjects in an enjoyable way.

4. **Collaboration**
    Team-oriented challenges that highlight teamwork, cooperation, and shared responsibilities.

5. **Communication**
    Exercises designed to enhance effective communication skills such as active listening and clear expression of thoughts.

6. **Creativity**
    Challenges that inspire participants to think outside the box, promoting fresh perspectives and innovative ideas.

7. Problem-solving

Activities that prompt participants to analyze situations critically from multiple angles and devise innovative solutions.

Online training activities

Activities marked with the mouse symbol ⌐ can be modified for online training.

ICEBREAKER

1. RECEPTION LINE

Participants form two lines and take turns asking their partners icebreaker questions. Afterward, they switch partners and ask a different question.

Purpose: Introduction, build rapport, and spark conversations.

Time required: 10 minutes.

Number of participants: 10 to 20.

Space required: Small.

Preparation: A set of icebreaker questions.

Conduct:

1. Split the group into two, forming two lines, A and B, facing each other.

2. Pose the first question, and individuals discuss it with their partner opposite them.

3. Afterward, the first person in line A moves to the opposite end of line A, and everyone in that line shifts down one spot, ensuring everyone has a new partner.

4. Proceed to ask the next question and repeat the process.

5. Continue until everyone from both lines has met each other.

2. BUDDIES HUNT

Participants mingle with others in search of individuals who share similarities with them.

Purpose: Encourage interaction, inject energy, and build connections.

Time required: 15 minutes.

Number of participants: 20 to 50.

Space required: Large.

Preparation: Prepare a sheet containing 10 to 15 "get-to-know-you" questions for each person.

Conduct:

1. Hand out the sheet to each person.

2. They have 5 minutes to answer the questions individually.

3. Afterward, they will have 10 minutes to interact with others and find individuals who have the same answers. They should then write down the names of those people.

4. To encourage mingling, they can only write down the name of each person once.

Sample questions:

1. What is your favorite food?

2. What is your favorite holiday destination?

3. What is your favorite movie?

4. What was the last movie you watched in the theatre?

5. Name one hobby you enjoy.

6. Name one sport you play.

7. Do you prefer coffee or tea?

8. Are you more of a morning person or a night person?

9. How long have you been working with the company?

10. What is your favorite place in the office?

3. FACTS BAG 🔖

Participants write a secret about themselves on a card and place it in a bag. The trainer randomly selects a card, reads the facts out, and the group tries to guess who it belongs to.

Purpose: Spark conversations, liven up atmosphere, and discover new things about others.

Time required: 15 minutes.

Number of participants: 10 to 15.

Space required: Small.

Preparation: Blank cards/papers and writing materials for each person.

Conduct:

1. Pass out the cards/paper to each person and have them write something about themselves that nobody else in the room knows.

2. Put all the cards in a bag.

3. Mix the cards in the bag, draw one randomly, and read the fact out loud.

4. Let the group try to guess who the fact belongs to.

5. After a few rounds of guessing, ask the person who wrote the fact to reveal themselves and explain it.

4. TWO TRUTHS AND A LIE 🖐

Every person shares three statements about themselves where one is a lie.

Purpose: Liven up the atmosphere, encourage participation, and discover new things about others.

Time required: 15 minutes.

Number of participants: 5 to 15.

Space required: Small.

Preparation: None.

Conduct:

1. Each person is to come up with two true and one false statement about themselves.

2. Make sure all the statements are equally believable to make them more interesting.

3. Give the group approximately 2 minutes to think about their statements.

4. Start by asking for a volunteer to share their three statements.

5. The rest of the group will then guess which statement is false.

6. Ask some of the guessing participants to explain their reasoning to encourage more interaction.

7. Once everyone has made their guess, reveal which statement was the lie.

5. HOW LIKELY ARE YOU TO 🖱

Individuals are given different situations and asked to select their responses from a set of options, where their choices may differ from those of others.

Purpose: Sparks conversation, appreciate others, and discover new things about others.

Time required: 15 minutes.

Number of participants: 8 to 15.

Space required: Small.

Preparation:

1. Mark out seven areas in the room, each representing a point on a 7-point Likert scale, for instance, from "very likely," to "very unlikely."

2. Prepare a list of questions with a 7-point scale response, such as, "How likely are you to start conversations with strangers?".

3. The response choices can vary for different questions, but should all be over a 7-point Likert scale.

Conduct:

1. Explain to the participants what the 7 markers represent.

2. Display the first question.

3. Tell them to stand near the marker that corresponds to their response.

4. Facilitate a discussion about the participants' answers to each question.

5. Move on to the next question and repeat the process.

6. MEET ME BINGO

Participants mingle with others and try to find people who match the descriptions on their Bingo sheet.

Purpose: Build rapport, encourage interaction, and inject energy.

Time required: 15 minutes.

Number of participants: 20 to 50.

Space required: Large.

Preparation: Print a Team Bingo board for each person.

Conduct:

1. Give each person a Bingo board.

2. The task is to find individuals who match the descriptions and write their names in the corresponding boxes.

3. Each name can only be written twice on each sheet. This rule encourages more social interaction.

4. The first person to get five in a row wins.

Bingo Board:

Speaks three different languages	Sang for money	Has broken a bone	Is afraid of heights	Has a tattoo
Had braces	Love to sing karaoke	Doesn't drink coffee	Ran a marathon	Has a pet
Loves math	Dislike chocolate	Born this month	Terrified of spiders	Has changed a tire
Likes spicy foot	Has no Facebook account	Is an only child	Plays a musical instrument	Exercise at least 3 times a week
Appeared on TV	Tried bungee jump	Is left-handed	Played sports professionally	Has ridden a horse

7. WHO AM I

Participants attempt to guess the identity of others by looking at pictures and interesting facts.

Purpose: Strengthen trust, appreciate others, and discover new things about others.

Time required: 15 minutes.

Number of participants: 8 to 15.

Space required: Small.

Preparation: Before the session, ask each person to provide a photo of something that represents them (but without themselves in it) and one interesting personal fact that the rest of the group may not know.

Conduct:

1. To make the activity last longer, have two rounds: one with photos and another with facts.

2. Share the first photos.

3. Ask the participants to guess who the person is and explain their reasoning.

4. Reveal the identity of the person and let them talk about the photo or facts.

5. Move on to the next set of photos and repeat the process.

8. SIMILARITIES AND DIFFERENCES⟟

Working in groups, participants discover something all have in common and something special that makes each person unique.

Purpose: Introduction, build connections, and encourage participation.

Time required: 15 minutes.

Number of participants: 5 to 10 per group.

Space required: Small.

Preparation: Writing materials.

Conduct:

1. Ask each group to find something that all members have in common.

2. The similarity should be interesting and provide insights about the group. Avoid obvious things like physical appearance or common knowledge.

3. Once all the groups have found their similarities, each group will take turns sharing their similarity with the other groups.

4. Then, ask each group to identify something special or unique about each person in their group.

5. This might take longer than finding similarities, as it can be more challenging.

9. POSTCARDS 🖰

Participants share pictures to start conversations about their personal strengths and contributions.

Purpose: Introduction, appreciate others, and create a positive environment.

Time required: 15 minutes.

Number of participants: 8 to 15.

Space required: Small.

Preparation: Prepare approximately twice as many travel postcards or image cards as there are participants.

Conduct:

1. Lay the cards out on a table.

2. Have each participant choose a card that represents a personal strength or positive quality they bring to the team.

3. Ask a participant to hold up their card while the others try to guess why they chose it. This is a chance for everyone to hear positive feedback and insights from others.

4. Then, ask the participant to share how accurate the group's guesses were before revealing the true meaning of their card.

10. THIS OR THAT 🖱

Participants choose between two similar options to learn each other's preferences and find commonalities among the group.

Purpose: Build connections, inject energy, and encourage participation.

Time required: 10 minutes.

Number of participants: 10 to 50.

Space required: Medium to large.

Preparation: A list of choices such as movies or television and big parties or small gatherings.

Conduct:

1. Have participants choose between two similar options, like Breakfast or dinner?

2. Those who choose breakfast will gather on one side of the room, while those who choose dinner will gather on the other side.

3. Ask them to pair up with someone on their side and discuss their preferences.

4. Repeat the activity with another set of choices.

5. After each round, find a new partner on the same side and talk about what they like.

11. SHOW AND TELL🖱

Participants share an item of personal significance.

Purpose: Strengthen trust, appreciate others, and discover new things about others.

Time required: 15 minutes.

Number of participants: 8 to 15.

Space required: Small.

Preparation: Before the session, ask participants to bring at least one item that holds personal significance for them.

Conduct:

1. Participants take turns presenting their items to the group and explain why it is important to them.

12. QUESTION BALL

Pass a beach ball around the group and answer simple questions to introduce yourselves.

Purpose: Introduction, inject energy, and liven up the atmosphere.

Time required: 15 minutes.

Number of participants: 10 to 20.

Space required: Medium to large.

Preparation: Take a large beach ball and write various get-to-know-you questions all over it.

Conduct:

1. Have everyone stand in a circle with enough space to comfortably toss and catch the beach ball.

2. Ask for a volunteer.

3. Toss the ball to the volunteer and have them answer the question closest to their right thumb.

4. Then, ask the volunteer to toss the ball to someone else.

5. Repeat the process until everyone has had a chance to answer a question.

13. QUESTIONS FOR ANOTHER GROUP ⊙

Participants work in teams and create questions to learn more about members of other groups.

Purpose: Encourage interaction, spark conversations, and discover new things about others.

Time required: 15 minutes.

Number of participants: 4 to 5 per group.

Space required: Small.

Preparation: Flipchart paper and writing materials for each group.

Conduct:

1. Create at least two groups.

2. The task is to come up with 5 questions that will help them learn more about the other groups.

3. Write the questions on flipchart paper.

4. Encourage participants to relate their questions to the topics covered in the training.

5. If there are more than two groups, assign each group to another group.

6. Hand over the flipchart paper with the questions to the assigned group, and let them discuss and prepare their responses.

7. The group can choose to answer the questions individually or collectively as a team.

8. Each group will take turns presenting their responses.

14. ONE STEP FORWARD⛯

Participants will move forward by one step for each "Have you ever" question they answer with a "yes."

Purpose: Encourage participation and build connections.

Time required: 10 minutes.

Number of participants: 10 to 25 people.

Space required: 10 to 25 people.

Preparation:

- Place 10 markers between the starting and finishing lines, where the gap between each marker is one step.

- Prepare at least 20 ice-breaking questions starting with "Have you ever," such as: "Have you ever gone bungee jumping?"

Conduct:

1. Have the participants stand side by side behind the starting line.

2. Explain that you will ask a series of "Have you ever" questions.

3. If their answer is "yes," they should take a step forward towards the next marker; if "no," they remain in place.

4. Ask the first question and pause for a moment to see who steps forward.

5. Encourage interaction and banter among participants to make the activity fun.

6. Repeat the process with the next question.

7. End the activity when a few people have crossed the finishing line or when all questions have been asked.

15. CANVAS DROP

Teams compete to see which group can better remember the details of the other.

Purpose: Encourage interaction and liven up atmosphere.

Time required: 25 minutes.

Number of participants: 10 to 20 people.

Space required: Medium.

Preparation: A cloth big enough to cover half of the group.

Conduct:

1. List 3 simple things for participants to learn about each other: favorite food, movies, and holiday destination.

2. Ask participants to meet as many people as possible in 5 minutes and share information.

3. No recording of the information exchange is allowed.

4. Divide participants into two teams and explain the activity is a test of how well they remember the details of the other group members.

5. Give the teams time to share information about their opponents before starting the activity.

6. One volunteer from each team will hold the cloth separating the two groups so that neither group can see the other.

7. Both teams will send one person closer to the cloth.

8. Call out a category, for example, favorite food.

9. Drop the cloth. The first person to correctly guess their opponent's favorite food scores a point.

10. Keep going until everyone has had a turn to guess.

16. HELLO, MY NAME IS 👌

Participants describe themselves with an adjective that begins with the same letter as their name.

Purpose: Introduction, encourage participation, and inject energy.

Time required: 10 minutes.

Number of participants: 8 to 50.

Space required: Medium to large.

Preparation: Name tags and writing materials for each participant.

Conduct:

1. Each person chooses an adjective that describes them, and it must start with the same letter as their first name. For instance, "Joyful Jessica".

2. Everyone takes turns introducing themselves and explaining their adjectives.

3. If the group is large, divide the participants into teams of 10 to 15 people for the sharing activity.

4. Or, they can walk around the room and mingle with others.

17. VALUES SORT

This exercise helps participants identify and prioritize their most important values.

Purpose: Promote inclusivity, enhance self-awareness, and spark conversations.

Time required: 15 minutes.

Number of participants: 5 to 20.

Space required: Small.

Preparation:

- Create 30 cards with a list of common values for each participant.

- Include 4 to 5 blank cards for participants to write down any additional values not listed.

Conduct:

1. Give each participant a set of cards.

2. Individually sort through the deck and choose 10 values that matter most to them.

3. If some values are missing, write them on the blank cards.

4. After selecting 10 values, narrow it down to 5 that are the most significant to them.

5. Then, rank these 5 values in order of importance.

6. Finally, share their values ranking with others.

Common values:

1. Integrity
2. Honesty
3. Respect
4. Responsibility
5. Empathy
6. Compassion
7. Kindness
8. Gratitude
9. Authenticity
10. Trustworthiness
11. Loyalty
12. Fairness
13. Generosity
14. Patience
15. Perseverance
16. Humility
17. Open-mindedness
18. Independence
19. Courage
20. Determination
21. Family
22. Friendship
23. Personal growth
24. Creativity
25. Balance
26. Teamwork
27. Innovation
28. Justice
29. Learning
30. Adventure

ENERGIZER

18. FIND SOMEONE WHO

Participants quickly rush to form groups with the person whom the trainer describes.

Purpose: Encourage participation and spontaneity, enhance focus, and increase energy level.

Time required: 10 minutes.

Number of participants: 15 to 50.

Space required: Medium to large.

Preparation: None.

Conduct:

1. Participants to walk around casually, shaking their limbs and relaxing.

2. The trainer will call out "Find someone..." and specify a clothing color or other visible traits.

3. The participants must quickly gather in groups with the person who matches the description.

4. Each group should not exceed 4 people, including the person being described.

5. Participants who fail to form a group will receive one strike.

6. If someone accumulates three strikes, they will be required to perform for the rest of the group.

7. Repeat this activity multiple times, each time using various clothing colors or characteristics.

19. FINGER CATCH

Participants will attempt to catch another person's finger while also avoiding having their own fingers caught by someone else.

Purpose: Enhance focus and encourage participation.

Time required: 10 minutes.

Number of participants: 8 to 50.

Space required: Medium to large.

Preparation: None.

Conduct:

1. Gather the group in a circle.

2. Everyone will extend their left hand with the palm open and facing upwards.

3. Next, extend their right hand, pointing the index finger downwards, towards the middle of the person on the right's open palm. Maintain a 5-inch gap between their index finger and the other person's palm.

4. The aim of this activity is to touch the palm of the person on their right with their index finger as many times as possible in 5 minutes without being caught.

5. At the same time, they need to catch the index finger of the person on their left who is attempting to touch their palm.

6. The hand with the palm cannot move upward to catch the finger; it can only open and close.

20. FIND THE LEADER

Participants follow a secret leader's movements, and the guesser must figure out who the leader is among them.

Purpose: Break monotony, encourage spontaneity, and enhance focus.

Time required: 10 minutes.

Number of participants: 15 to 50.

Space required: Medium to large.

Preparation: None.

Conduct:

1. Gather the group in a circle.

2. One person is selected as the guesser and temporarily leaves the room.

3. While the guesser is away, the group chooses a leader.

4. The leader will perform simple actions that the rest of the group can quickly imitate, like scratching their head or hopping on one foot.

5. When the guesser returns to the room, their task is to figure out who the leader is by observing the group's movements.

6. If the group is large, form a team of 2 to 3 guessers.

21. LINE UP

Participants arrange themselves in a line based on categories such as their birthdays or height.

Purpose: Encourage participation and build camaraderie.

Time required: 10 minutes.

Number of participants: 8 to 15.

Space required: Medium.

Preparation:

- Use chalk, rope, or tape to mark a line on the floor.
- Create a list of categories for the group to organize themselves.

Conduct:

1. Ask everyone to stand on the line with both feet facing you.

2. The task is to rearrange themselves based on your instructions. For example, tallest to shortest.

3. Emphasize that they must always keep one foot on the line. If anyone loses contact with the line, the whole group starts over.

4. Start with a simple category, like ordering them by height, to help them understand the activity.

5. Introduce a no-talking rule to make it more challenging.

22. CIRCLE THE CIRCLE

Participants form a circle, holding hands, then pass a hula hoop around the circle as fast as they can without letting go of each other's hands.

Purpose: Encourage spontaneity, enhance focus, and inject humor.

Time required: 10 minutes.

Number of participants: 15 to 50.

Space required: Medium to large.

Preparation:

-   Get some lively music ready along with a sound system to play during the activity.

-   Hula hoops.

Conduct:

1. Have the group form a circle and hold hands.

2. Put 1 hula hoop between any two people's arms. If the group is larger, add 2 hoops between different pairs of people on other sides of the circle.

3. The task is to pass the hula hoop around the circle in a clockwise direction. Participants should slide the hoops through their bodies while still holding hands.

4. When the background music stops, the person who is left holding the hoops will sit out for the next round.

5. Repeat this process for a few more rounds.

6. Those who sat out will be "penalized".

23. BIG WIND BLOWS

Participants must stand up and quickly find an empty chair to sit in when a shared characteristic is called out.

Purpose: Increase energy level, encourage participation and enhance focus.

Time required: 10 minutes.

Number of participants: 15 to 25.

Space required: Medium to large.

Preparation:

- Prepare enough chairs for everyone except one participant.
- Arrange the chairs in a circle, facing inward towards the middle.

Conduct:

1. Ask for a volunteer to start in the middle of the circle, while the rest of the participants sit on the chairs.

2. The person in the middle begins by saying, "Big wind blows for everyone who..." and then adds a statement, like "has a pet cat."

4. Anyone in the group who shares that characteristic (including the person in the middle) must stand up and quickly find a new seat that is at least 2 chairs away from their current one.

5. The person left standing without a seat now becomes the one in the middle and comes up with a new statement to complete the phrase, "Big wind blows for..."

6. The game continues this way until many group members have had a turn in the middle.

24. HANDSHAKE FRENZY

Participants try to find others with the same card values through handshakes. This activity can also be used to form groups quickly.

Purpose: Encourage participation and break monotony.

Time required: 10 minutes.

Number of participants: 20 to 50.

Space required: Medium to large.

Preparation:

- Prepare 1 poker card for each person.

- Jack represents the number 11, Queen 12, and King 13.

Conduct:

1. Hand out a card to each person and instruct them to look at their cards without revealing their values to others.

2. Their task is to find others who have cards with the same value (not suit) as theirs.

3. The only way to communicate is through handshakes, by shaking hands the same number of times as the value of their cards.

4. For example, if one person has a card with the number 4, and another person has a card with the number 7, they will shake hands at the same time. The first person will shake 4 times, and the second person will shake 7 times. By the fifth shake, they'll realize they don't have the same value. In this case, they'll find someone else to shake hands with.

5. When they find someone with the same value, they'll stay together and continue to look for others with the same value.

25. COUNT UP ✌️

As a team, the participants must count from 1 to 30 within 60 seconds without repeating any numbers. Though it might seem simple, the rules make it challenging for the team to coordinate the count.

Purpose: Encourage spontaneity, enhance focus, and break monotony.

Time required: 5 minutes.

Number of participants: 15 to 25.

Space required: Small.

Preparation: None.

Conduct:

1. Arrange the group in a circle.

2. The goal is to count from 1 to 30 in less than 60 seconds.

3. Each person must say at least one number.

4. Nobody can say more than two numbers.

5. No one is allowed to count sequentially like '1, 2'.

6. The person seated or standing next to the last 'counter' cannot continue the count.

7. No talking or writing during the activity.

8. If a number is repeated or any rule is broken, restart the activity.

26. SCAVENGER HUNT ✎

Participants work in teams to find specific items that are called out.

Time required: 15 minutes.

Purpose: Encourage spontaneity, increase energy level, and build camaraderie.

Number of participants: 25 to 50.

Space required: Small.

Preparation: None.

Conduct:

1. Organizing this game as a team competition to encourage participation.

2. Even though scavenger hunts are commonly played, explain the rules briefly to ensure everyone understands how the game works.

3. Participants will work in teams to search for the specific items you announce in their bags or around the room.

4. The first team to hand you the correct items will earn a point.

5. The team with the most points wins.

6. Point out any safety hazards, like table corners or bags on the floor, that participants might overlook in the excitement of the game.

27. HIGH FIVE, LOW FIVE

This activity will quickly get a big group of people moving and mingling with each other by exchanging high and low fives with one another.

Purpose: Increase energy level and encourage interaction.

Time required: 5 minutes.

Number of participants: 15 to 50.

Space required: Medium to large.

Preparation: None.

Conduct:

1. Demonstrate a high five and say something nice to the person you are high fiving.

2. When you say "go", everyone should high five as many people as possible in 1 minute and exchange friendly words with each person they high five.

3. After that, demonstrate the low five - intentionally miss a high five, but then continue swinging the arm to contact the other person's palm at waist level and say something nice to each other.

4. When you say "go", everyone should exchange low fives and friendly words with people they haven't high five yet in 1 minute.

28. ROCK, PAPER, SCISSORS CONTEST

A fun twist on a classic game: the winners advance to the next round, and the losers become their fans. This continues until there's a final showdown with 2 players, each with a large cheering crowd behind them!

Purpose: Increase energy level, encourage playfulness and build camaraderie.

Time required: 10 minutes.

Number of participants: 15 to 50.

Space required: Medium to large.

Preparation: None.

Conduct:

1. Find a partner.

2. Play 'Rock, Paper, Scissors' against each other for 3 rounds until someone wins.

3. The winner finds a new opponent, and the loser becomes a fan of the winner.

4. The winner from the second game looks for a new opponent, while the losing team joins their fan base.

5. Repeat this process until only 2 players are left, each with a huge fan base cheering for them.

29. HUDDLE UP

Participants need to quickly group together based on the number that is called out.

Purpose: Increase energy level, enhance focus and encourage participation.

Time required: 5 minutes.

Number of participants: 15 to 50.

Space required: Medium to large.

Preparation: None.

Conduct:

1. Participants walk around and mingle with each other.

2. Trainer randomly announces a number.

3. Participants must quickly form groups with that number of members.

4. Anyone who can't find a group will receive a strike.

5. If someone gets three strikes, they will be "penalized".

30. NAME TAG CHASE

Participants must find their name tags while avoiding others trying to snatch the name tag from their back.

Purpose: Increase energy level, encourage spontaneity and playfulness.

Time required: 10 minutes.

Number of participants: 15 to 50.

Space required: Medium to large.

Preparation:

- Name tags and markers for every participant.

- 1 large bag.

Conduct:

1. Ask participants to write their names on a name tag and put it in a bag.

2. Arrange the participants in a circle.

3. Pass the bag around the circle and have each person draw a name tag from it.

4. The name tag they pick should not be their own or belong to the person on their right in the circle.

5. Instruct them to stick the name tag they drew onto the back of the person to their right.

6. When you say "go," everyone must move among the group and try to find their own name tag while avoiding someone else discovering the name tag stuck on their back.

7. Once a person finds their own name tag, they should take it off the person's back, display it on their chest for

everyone to see, and return to their original position in the circle.

31. IN, OUT, UP, DOWN

Participants do the opposite of what the trainer says.

Purpose: Inject humor, encourage participation and spontaneity.

Time required: 10 minutes.

Number of participants: 15 to 50.

Space required: Small to large.

Preparation: A list of actions that participants can safely perform within the given area.

Conduct:

1. Gather participants in a circle in a spacious area.

2. In a classroom or theatre-style setting, participants can simply stand up and remain in their current position.

3. Explain the actions they need to perform. For example, you'll say 'in' and they should jump into the circle; you'll say 'up' and they should stand up, and when you say 'down', they should squat.

4. Practice these simple instructions as a warm-up to familiarize everyone with the actions.

5. Now, explain that they need to do the opposite of what you say. For instance, when you say 'out', they should jump out of the circle; when you say 'down', they should stand up, and when you say 'up', they should squat.

32. GROUP POKER

Participants mingle with each other by finding other people who have playing cards that can help them form poker combinations.

Purpose: Enhance focus and increase energy level.

Time required: 10 minutes.

Number of participants: 25 to 50.

Space required: Medium to large.

Preparation:

- 1 poker card for each person.
- A presentation slide with information about poker combinations like Royal Flush, Full House, etc.

Conduct:

1. Give each participant a poker card randomly.
2. The goal is to find others with playing cards to create the called-out combinations.
3. Before starting, share the information on poker combinations so that everyone knows which card to look for to form combinations.
4. Keep the information displayed throughout the activity.
5. Anyone who can't find a group will receive a strike.
6. If someone gets three strikes, they will be "penalized".

33. YES, NO

Participants ask each other straightforward yes/no questions. When someone responds with a "Yes," they should shake their head. If the answer is "No," they should nod their head.

Purpose: Enhance focus, inject humor, and encourage interaction.

Time required: 10 minutes.

Number of participants: 15 to 50

Space required: Medium to large.

Preparation: 5 ice cream sticks for each person.

Conduct:

1. Give each person 5 ice cream sticks.

2. The goal is to give away as many ice cream sticks as possible by mingling with others individually and asking them simple yes or no questions. For example, "Is today Monday.

3. If the answerer says "Yes", they should shake their head; if they say "No", they should nod their head – opposite of their words.

4. If the answer or head movement is wrong, the questioner gives them an ice cream stick.

5. Then, the answerers get a turn to ask a question.

6. After both have asked each other questions, they find new partners.

7. Keep pairing up until the trainer calls time, even if they've given away their sticks.

TRAINING INTRODUCTION

34. RANDOM WORDS 🖰

Participants are challenged to connect a random word to the training topics.

Purpose: Stimulate creative thinking on the subject.

Time required: 15 minutes.

Number of participants: 8 to 15.

Space required: Small.

Preparation: Paper and writing materials.

Conduct:

1. Without providing an explanation for the activity's purpose, ask each participant to write a random word on a piece of paper.

2. Afterwards, they should crumple the paper and throw it to the front of the class.

3. Then, each person should pick up someone else's crumpled paper.

4. Participants need to find a way to connect the word they picked with the training topic and share their connection with the rest of the class.

5. While participants explain their connections, jot down relevant points on a flipchart for further discussion later.

35. WORD PLAY

Teams attempt to create as many words as they can that are related to the training, following the rules of Scrabble.

Purpose: Foster group discussion on the topic.

Time required: 15 minutes.

Number of participants: 2 to 3 per group.

Space required: Small.

Preparation: Prepare a grid sheet measuring 20 by 30 squares and writing materials for each team.

Conduct:

1. Separate the participants into two or more groups.

2. Provide each team with a grid sheet.

3. The task is to create as many words as possible related to the training topic in 10 minutes.

4. Teams can use an unlimited number of letters.

5. However, the regular Scrabble rules must be followed:

    1. All words must be in a single horizontal row or a single vertical column.

    2. New words must connect to the existing words.

    3. Words must be found in the dictionary.

6. Begin with a word related to the training topic, writing it across the center of the grid.

7. When the time is up, teams will exchange papers and evaluate each other's work.

8. Evaluating teams can question the relevance of the words, and the other team should justify their choices. Encourage a lively debate to foster interaction on the topic.

9. As the teams debate, take note of the relevant points on a flipchart for later discussion.

36. LOGO QUIZ 🖱

Participants guess the meaning or name of logos, signs, or symbols.

Purpose: Raise awareness of images related to the training.

Time required: 10 minutes.

Number of participants: 2 to 3 per group.

Space required: Small

Preparation: Create a worksheet with logos or signs that are relevant to the training.

Conduct:

1. Separate the participants into two or more groups.

2. Provide each team with a worksheet and writing materials.

3. Allow 10 minutes for the teams to name the logos.

4. Encourage them to look for answers in the training materials.

5. The team that correctly names the most logos wins.

37. ANAGRAMS ⊕

Participants are challenged to create words using letters from a selected text.

Purpose: Introduce important words or phrases.

Time required: 10 minutes.

Number of participants: 2 to 5 per group.

Space required: Small.

Preparation:

- A long word or phrase related to the training topic.
- Writing materials.

Conduct:

1. Create at least two groups.
2. The task is to create as many words as possible using only the letters from the given text.
3. Each team should write down their words on the provided paper or whiteboard.
4. Allow 5 minutes for teams to form the words.
5. When the time is up, have teams compare and verify each other's answers.

38. TEAM TRIVIA CHALLENGE ⛥

Teams compete to test their knowledge on the training subjects.

Purpose: Test participants' subject knowledge.

Time required: 10 minutes.

Number of participants: 2 to 5 per group.

Space required: Small.

Preparation:

- Prepare quiz questions on slides.

- Answer buzzer for each team.

Conduct:

1. Split the participants into two or more groups.

2. Training-related questions will appear on the screen, one at a time.

3. The first team to press the buzzer gets the chance to answer. If they answer incorrectly, other teams can attempt to answer.

4. Each correct answer earns the team 10 points.

5. To discourage teams from rushing to press the buzzer, they will receive a 10-point penalty for answering incorrectly.

6. Participants are challenged to create words using letters from a selected text.

39. CROSSWORD PUZZLE🖱

This activity is a fun way to introduce participants to important training terms.

Purpose: Encourage group discussion on the topic.

Time required: 10 minutes.

Number of participants: 2 to 3 per group

Space required: Small.

Preparation:

-   Use an online crossword puzzle maker to create the puzzle.

-   Include at least 15 questions to increase engagement.

Conduct:

1. Divide the participants into two or more groups.

2. Give the teams 10 minutes to complete the puzzle.

3. Encourage them to use the training materials to find answers.

4. The team with the most correct answers wins.

40. MYSTERY BOX 🖱

Participants randomly select an item from a mystery box and then try to figure out its importance and how it relates to the training.

Purpose: Stimulate reflection on the subject.

Time required: 15 minutes.

Number of participants: 8 to 15.

Space required: Small.

Preparation: Prepare training-related images or words, write them on separate pieces of paper, and place them in a box.

Conduct:

1. Participants will take turns drawing an item from the box and guessing its relevance and connection to the training.

41. SKETCHARY ✋

Participants become acquainted with the game by playing this classic draw and guess game.

Purpose: Generate enthusiasm for the topic.

Time required: 15 minutes.

Number of participants: 3 to 7 per group.

Space required: Small.

Preparation:

- Prepare a list of training-related words for the participants to draw.

- Drawing materials.

Conduct:

1. Create at least two groups.

2. Each team designates one person to draw while the others guess.

3. The drawer receives a word to draw but cannot use gestures or spell it out.

4. The team has 1 minute to guess the word.

5. If the team guesses correctly, they earn a point. If not, the other team can attempt to guess and steal a point.

6. After that, the other team takes their turn for the next round.

COLLABORATION

42. ORCHESTRA

Participants are split into groups, and each group picks a sound for their instrument. Then, a conductor tries to make music using those chosen instruments.

Purpose: Encourage synergy and cohesiveness.

Time required: 10 minutes.

Number of participants: 20 to 50.

Space required: Small.

Preparation: None.

Conduct:

1. Split the participants into 4 or more groups.

2. Tell each group they will create an instrument using their hands or feet, like clapping or stomping.

3. Each group must come up with a unique sound that is different from the others.

4. One participant will be the conductor and try to make music.

5. Whenever the conductor points at a group, they will play their sound.

43. PROJECT PIPELINE

Participants collaborate to build a system using PVC pipes to transfer a set of tennis balls.

Purpose: Improve group planning skills and coordinated teamwork.

Time required: 20 minutes.

Number of participants: 5 to 8 per group.

Space required: Medium to large.

Preparation:

- Place a starting line and use a bucket or hula hoop as the endpoint where the balls will be collected. Ensure that the two points are at least 8 yards apart.

- Get 6 PVC pipes, each 3 feet long and with a diameter of at about 3 inches, for each group. Make sure that all the pipes have the same length and diameter.

- Provide each team with 6 tennis balls.

Conduct:

1. Create two or more teams.

2. The objective of this activity is to build a system using pipes to transport all the balls and safely deposited them into the container at the end point.

3. Hold 2 pipes side by side to form a channel through which the balls can roll. Then, hold another 2 pipes at the end to establish a continuous flow.

4. The balls cannot go through the pipes; they can only roll on the surface of the pipes.

5. Each team decides how many balls they want to move at a time.

6. No one is allowed to touch the balls at any point, except at the starting point when placing the balls on the pipes to begin the activity.

7. Any ball that falls to the ground will be reset and placed back at the starting point.

8. The team that successfully transfers all the balls in the shortest time will be the winner.

44. ELECTRIC FENCE

Participants collaborate to help each other cross the electric fence without touching it.

Purpose: Strengthen trust, collaboration, and team cohesion.

Time required: 25 minutes.

Number of participants: 10 to 20.

Space required: Medium to large.

Preparation:

- Set up the "fence" by firmly attaching two ropes to the wall or stands.
- The first rope should be 3 feet high, and the second rope should be 5 feet high.

Conduct:

1. The group must work together as a team to safely move everyone over or through the fence without touching it.
2. They are not allowed to cross under the fence.
3. If any part of a person's body touches the "Fence" while crossing, they will have to start over.
4. If the people supporting someone touch the fence, the person being supported will have to start over.
5. Team members can lift and support each other to pass over or through the "Fence."
6. Demonstrate how to lift and support safely before starting, and watch participants as they cross at heights.

45. SNEAK A PEAK

Participants try to recreate a Lego model with limited visibility and must rely on each other's memory.

Purpose: Foster personal accountability.

Time required: 20 minutes.

Number of participants: 3 to 4 per group.

Space required: Medium.

Preparation:

- Create a multilayer Lego structure and ensure there are enough Lego bricks to recreate the same structure.

- Designate a holding area for the teams to gather and a location to conceal the Lego model.

Conduct:

1. Split the participants into 2 or more teams.

2. Hide the Lego model from view.

3. Each team member will take turns approaching the hidden Lego model and have a 5-second glimpse of it.

4. After seeing the structure, the team member will return to the holding area, where loose bricks are provided, and start building a replica based on their memory.

5. This process continues until the team successfully completes building the replica.

6. The first team to successfully replicate the model wins.

46. TEAM BALLERS

This is an indoor activity similar to team sports, where teams score points by maneuvering balloons into hula hoops.

Purpose: Improve group planning skills and coordination.

Time required: 20 minutes.

Number of participants: 5 to 8 per group.

Space required: Medium.

Preparation:

- Arrange one hula hoop for each team and place them on the floor, approximately 10 yards away from the starting line.

- Prepare 10 balloons for each team.

Conduct:

1. Divide the participants into 2 or more teams.

2. The task for each team is to move the balloons, one at a time, from the start line and land them in the hula hoop.

3. During the transfer, each team member must hit the balloon exactly twice, no more, no less. If any member fails to do so, the team will have to restart with that balloon.

4. If the balloon touches the floor outside of the hoop during the transfer, the team will have to restart with that balloon.

5. Once a balloon lands in the hula hoop, the team then return to the start line and begin moving the next balloon.

6. The team earns 10 points for each balloon that successfully lands inside the hoop.

7. Balloons that land in the hula hoop are not required to remain inside.

47. THUMB WRESTLING

This is a thumb-wrestling game with a twist. Instead of trying to beat each other, players need to work together with their partners to win.

Purpose: Promote a Win-Win mindset.

Time required: 5 minutes.

Number of participants: 2 per group.

Space required: Small.

Preparation: None.

Conduct:

1. Have everyone pair up. They can do this activity while standing or seated.

2. Ask for a volunteer to demonstrate the activity with you.

3. Grip the volunteer's hand as if you were thumb wrestling, but avoid using the term "thumb-wrestling".

4. Every time they press their partner's thumb down with their own thumb, they earn 1 point.

5. They have 1 minute to score as many points as possible.

6. Demonstrate the activity with the volunteer, who will likely be in a competitive mode, which is a natural reaction.

7. Start the activity without giving participants time to plan.

8. When the time is up, ask the group how many points they have scored.

9. In most cases, participants will report low numbers, but they could have scored higher if they collaborated by taking turns to press each other's thumb.

48. DESERT SURVIVAL 🖱

In this group decision-making exercise, participants will individually rank a set of items based on their significance for surviving in the desert. Afterwards, they will collectively rank the items as a group.

Purpose: Encourage collective decision-making and improve conflict resolution skills.

Time required: 20 minutes.

Number of participants: 4 to 8 per group.

Space required: Small.

Preparation: Prepare 1 copy of the Survival Ranking Sheet and writing materials for each participant.

Conduct:

1. Hand out 1 Ranking Sheet to each participant

2. Read out the scenario.

3. Explain the task - rank the 14 items according to their importance to your survival, starting with "1" the most important, to "14" the least important.

4. Allocate 5 minutes to the participants to complete the ranking individually.

5. Subsequently, divide them into groups of 5 to 10 people.

6. Allocate 15 minutes to the groups to collaboratively discuss and rank the items.

Scenario:

It is 10:00 A.M. in the summer and you have just crash-landed in the middle of the Sahara Desert. You and your fellow passengers survived but unfortunately, the pilot did not. The plane has completely burned and only the airplane frame remains. Everyone is dressed in lightweight clothing—short-sleeved shirts, pants, socks, and street shoes, everyone has a handkerchief. While scavenging the area, the group salvaged 14 items in the wreckage that could prove helpful.

Ranking sheet:

Items	Ranking	Ranking
1. Flashlight (4 battery size)		
2. Jackknife		
3. Sectional air map of the area		
4. Plastic raincoat (large size)		
5. Magnetic Compass		
6. Compress kit with gauze		
7. 45 caliber pistol (loaded)		
8. Parachute (red & white)		
9. 1 quart of water per person		
10. 2 quarts of 80 proof Vodka		
11. A pair of sunglasses per person		
12. A cosmetic mirror		
13. 1 top coat per person		
14. Book titled 'Edible Animals of the Desert'		

Ranking by military experts:

1. Cosmetic Mirror - A powerful tool to show your presence.

2. 1 Top Coat Per Person - Helps retain moisture and prevent perspiration loss.

3. 1 Quart of Water Per Person - For temporary hydration.

4. Flashlight (4 battery size) - A reliable device for night signaling.

5. Parachute (red and white) - Provides shelter and can be used as a signaling device.

6. Jackknife - Useful for cutting cacti for water and rigging.

7. Plastic Raincoat (large size) - Can collect moisture overnight when placed over a hole.

8. 45 Caliber Pistol (loaded) - To use as a sounding signal.

9. A Pair of Sunglasses Per Person - Protects eyes from intense sunlight.

10. Compress Kit with Gauze - Useful for various purposes in the intense desert environment.

11. Magnetic compass - Not very helpful for navigation, staying near the crash site is advised.

12. Sectional Air Map of the area - Of limited use, can be used for starting a fire or other needs.

13. A Book Entitled "Edible Animals of the Desert" - Dehydration is a more critical concern than starvation, and hunting can lead to water loss.

14. 2 Quarts of 80 Proof Vodka - Little value as alcohol dehydrates the body.

49. MOONBALL

Participants work together to keep a big inflatable beach ball for a certain duration.

Purpose: Foster personal accountability and coordinated teamwork.

Time required: 15 minutes.

Number of participants: 8 to 15.

Space required: Medium to large.

Preparation: 1 large inflatable beach ball.

Conduct:

1. Gather the participants in a circle.

2. The objective is to keep the beach ball in the air for a duration of 3 minutes.

3. Each participant can only use one hand to hit the ball and keep it from touching the ground.

4. No one can hit the ball twice in a row.

5. Every individual must hit the ball at least twice during the 3-minute time period.

50. SHOE TOWER

Participants work in teams to construct the tallest shoe tower while racing against the clock.

Purpose: Encourage collaboration with speed and agility.

Time required: 10 minutes.

Number of participants: 5 to 10 per group.

Space required: Small to medium.

Preparation: None.

Conduct:

1. Separate the participants into two or more teams.

2. The task is to build a free-standing tower with only the shoes of group members.

3. The tower must stand on its own for at least 20 seconds.

4. If the tower falls, the team needs to start over.

5. Complete the activity within 3 minutes.

6. The group with the tallest tower wins.

7. If there's only one group, set different height targets to challenge them.

51. OCTOPUS DOODLE

Participants will operate a writing tool together as a team to write words or draw images.

Purpose: Foster team cohesion.

Time required: 10 minutes.

Number of participants: 5 to 8 per group.

Space required: Small to medium.

Preparation:

- Create the writing tool by wrapping tying an equal number of twines around a marker as there are people in each group.
- A large piece of writing paper for each group.

Conduct:

1. Team will use the writing device to write words or draw images according to the trainer's instructions.

2. Each member must hold onto one end of the twine.

3. No one should touch the paper or the marker.

52. FOOTZA

The goal of this team activity is to build the tallest tower using only their feet.

Purpose: Improve group planning skills and emphasize effective resource management.

Time required: 5 minutes.

Number of participants: 10 to 15 per group.

Space required: Small to medium.

Preparation: None.

Conduct:

1. Create at least 2 teams.

2. The task is to build the tallest tower using only the team members' feet, under these rules:

    -   The feet must stay connected throughout the process.

    -   The feet must remain in position for 10 seconds.

3. Complete the activity within 3 minutes.

4. Participants can lift each other to connect their feet but cannot use any furniture or the wall for support.

5. Pay attention to the safety of the participants, especially when some are being lifted.

53. TURNING POINT

While standing on a tarp, teams must flip it over without anyone touching the ground.

Purpose: Foster cross-functional collaboration and Win-Win mindset.

Time required: 15 minutes.

Number of participants: 3 to 5 per group.

Space required: Medium to large.

Preparation: Get each team a tarp that can fit 5 to 6 people standing with some room to move around.

Conduct:

1. Create at least two teams.

2. Give each team a tarp and ask them to stand on it.

3. The task is to flip the tarp over without anyone stepping on the ground.

4. They can't use the wall, floor, or furniture for support.

5. As the teams struggle to flip the tarp, nudge them to collaborate with each other instead of competing.

6. The best solution is for teams to share their tarps. Members from one team should move to the other team's tarp, making it easier to flip the original team's tarp.

54. LOOSE CHANGE

This is a fun and fast activity involving people coming together to form groups of different values.

Purpose: Demonstrate that each team member is valuable, no matter their role.

Time required: 5 minutes.

Number of participants: 15 to 50.

Space required: Large.

Preparation: None.

Conduct:

1. Split the group into two based on easily distinguishable physical characteristics, like hair length or shirt color.

2. Give each member from the larger group a value of 10 cents, and those from the smaller group a value of 5 cents.

3. The task is to form groups based on the value you call.

4. Participants can create groups with people with the same or opposite values. For instance, two 10-cent members and two 5-cent members can team up to form 30 cents.

5. Keep track of the groups after each round. Participants who fail to form the correct value will receive a strike.

6. Those who receive three strikes will be "penalized".

7. At the beginning, call out values ending with zero, like 40 cents and 60 cents.

8. In later rounds, call out values ending with 5 cents. This will make participants rush to team up with those who have lower values.

55. SPIDER'S WED

Participants collaborate to help each other navigate across a spider's web without touching it.

Purpose: Strengthen trust, foster big-picture thinking, and improve group planning skills.

Time required: 25 minutes.

Number of participants: 15 to 50.

Space required: Medium to large.

Preparation:

- Make the spider's web using twines or ropes and create holes of different sizes.
- Secured the spider's web firmly to the walls or stands.

Conduct:

1. The group must work together as a team to safely move everyone from one side of the web to the other without touching it.
2. If any part of a person's body touches the web while crossing, they will have to start over.
3. If the people supporting someone contact the spider web, the person being supported will have to start over.
4. Team members can lift and support each other to pass through the higher holes.
5. Demonstrate how to lift and support safely before starting the activity, and watch participants as they cross at heights.
6. Put a limit on the number of members allowed to cross a specific hole so that not everyone takes the easiest route.

56. A TO Z SCAVENGER HUNT ✎

Participants search for objects that start with each letter from A to Z.

Purpose: Encourage effective planning and delegation.

Time required: 15 minutes.

Number of participants: 4 to 6 per group.

Space required: Medium to large.

Preparation: None.

Conduct:

1. Split the participants into teams to create a competitive atmosphere.

2. The task is to search for objects in their bags and the room that starts with each letter from A to Z, and organize the items in alphabetical order.

3. Each correct item earns the team one point.

57. PEGS TOWER

Participants work in teams to construct the tallest tower using only clothes pegs.

Purpose: Encourage collaboration, effective use of resources, and creative thinking.

Time required: 15 minutes.

Number of participants: 2 to 3 per group.

Space required: Small.

Preparation:

- 50 to 100 wooden clothes peg for each team.
- Tables for the team to build the tower on.

Conduct:

1. Split the participants into teams to create a sense of competition.
2. The task is to build a self-supporting tower using only the pegs.
3. The tower needs to pass a wind test, which you will fan a magazine at it to check its strength.
4. The team has 10 minutes to complete the activity.
5. The team with the tallest tower that passes the wind test wins.

58. BLINDFOLD SQUARES

Participants collaborate to create squares using ropes while blindfolded.

Purpose: Improve group planning skills and promote personal accountability and coordinated teamwork.

Time required: 40 minutes.

Number of participants: 4 to 6 per group.

Space required: Large.

Preparation:

- 1 blindfold for each person.

- An 18-foot-long rope for each team.

Conduct:

1. This activity works best with multiple groups involved, although it can be done with just one team.

2. The task is to create squares using ropes.

3. Participants will be blindfolded throughout the activity, but not during the planning phase.

4. Once blindfolded, they will be shuffled around the room.

5. The rope will be placed on the floor for each group to find.

6. All members must keep touching the ropes while forming the square.

7. Make sure to give them enough time to strategize.

8. Explain the potential hazards to the group before starting.

9. To make it more challenging, teams can only communicate using animal sounds and/or form overlapping squares with other groups.

59. ARRANGE THE CARDS

In teams, participants collaborate to arrange playing cards in a specific order.

Purpose: Encourage coordinated teamwork and effective delegation.

Time required: 10 minutes.

Number of participants: 3 to 4 per group.

Space required: Small.

Preparation:

- 1 deck of playing cards for each team.

- Tables for teams to arrange their cards.

Conduct:

1. Split the participants into 2 or more teams.

2. The task is to arrange the cards exactly as they are shown.

3. Place all the cards neatly in rows without any of them touching.

4. The team that completes the task the quickest will be the winner.

5. There's no separate planning time; instead, the teams will have 5 minutes to plan and execute their strategy.

6. The main point is to see how effectively the teams use their time.

60. HELIUM STICK

Participants must work together to synchronize their movements and move a stick.

Purpose: Encourage cohesive and coordinated teamwork.

Time required: 15 minutes.

Number of participants: 5 to 10 per group.

Space required: Medium.

Preparation: 1 long, thin, and lightweight rod for each team that doesn't bend easily.

Conduct:

1. Arrange team members in two rows, facing each other.

2. The goal is to lower the Helium Stick from a height of 4.5 yards to 4 inches above the ground and then raise it back to the starting height of 4 inches.

3. The Stick will be placed on top of each member's index finger, and that will be the only point of contact.

4. All members must keep in contact with the Stick at all times.

5. If anyone's finger is not touching the Stick or they touch it with a finger other than the index finger, the task will be restarted.

61. GROUP JUGGLE

The aim of this activity is to work together as a team and juggle a set of balls.

Purpose: Foster team cohesion and patience for others. Number of participants: 8 to 15.

Time required: 15 minutes.

Space required: Medium to large.

Preparation: 1 one tennis or soft squashy ball for each person.

Conduct:

1. Form a circle with everyone standing arm's length apart. Stay in this formation during the activity.

2. Give each participant 1 ball.

3. The goal is for the group to juggle the balls together. Each person should toss their ball to the person on their right and catch the ball thrown to them by the person on their left, simultaneously.

4. Use the same hand to toss and catch the ball, but participants can choose which hand they prefer. Once chosen, they must stick to that hand throughout the activity.

5. If any ball is dropped or someone fails to catch a ball with their hand, the task will restart.

62. KEY PUNCH

In teams, participants need to touch number plates that are randomly placed in a specific order.

Time required: 30 minutes.

Purpose: Improve group planning skills and foster personal accountability.

Number of participants: 5 to 7 per group.

Space required: Large.

Preparation:

- Mark out a 9 x 12 feet rectangle and arrange 30 paper plates inside it. These plates should be numbered sequentially but placed randomly within the rectangle.
- Additionally, find a separate area, away from the view of the plates, where the participants can gather.

Conduct:

1. Create 2 or more teams.

2. Each group must touch the plates sequentially from 1 to 30 as quickly as possible, under these rules:

    - A 5-second penalty will be given if two people are inside the rectangle at the same time.

    - Every team member must touch at least one plate. If this rule is violated, the team will start again from the smallest number, but the time will continue to count.

    - The plates must be touched in the correct order. If this rule is violated, the team will start again from the smallest number, but the time will continue to count.

3. You will keep track of the total time taken for each attempt.

4. Each team will have 3 attempts to improve their timing.

5. Shuffle the number plates after each round without informing the teams.

6. The teams will take turns alternately during their attempts.

7. After each attempt, the team will move to a holding area to strategize for the next round while the next team takes its turn.

63. INTERLINK

The challenge is to create a device with twine to transfer a ball.

Time required: 30 minutes.

Purpose: Encourage effective communication and coordinated teamwork.

Number of participants: 6 to 8 per group.

Space required: Large.

Preparation:

- Mark a starting point and an ending point, with approximately 20 yards between them.
- Get a tennis ball size, lightweight plastic ball for each team.
- Provide each participant with a 2-foot-long twine.

Conduct:

1. The group's task is to move the ball from the starting point to the endpoint using a device resembling a spider's web made with twine.

2. To create the device, place one piece of twine on top of another on the floor. Arrange them in a way that resembles a ship's steering wheel with several spokes.

3. The twine must not be woven through each other.

4. Each participant will hold the ends of two twines, one in each hand.

5. When all participants stand up together, the web device will form.

6. One participant should place the ball in the middle of the device to start the transportation.

7. The task will restart if the ball is dropped.

64. PROJECT ROLLERCOASTER

Build a roller coaster together as a team.

Purpose: Boost teamwork, improve group planning and stimulate creative thinking.

Time required: 45 minutes.

Number of participants: 4 to 7 per group.

Space required: Medium to large.

Preparation:

- A set of materials for each team containing 1 tennis ball, stationery items like scissors and sticky tape, and construction materials such as straws, balloon sticks, balloon stick holders, newspaper, ice cream sticks, etc.

- Tables that are at least 4.5 feet long for building the roller coaster.

Conduct:

1. The aim of this activity is to construct a self-supporting roller coaster using the given materials.

2. The roller coaster should allow a tennis ball (acting as a carriage) to travel through it without any human intervention, except for releasing the ball at the starting point.

3. The roller coaster should consist of a minimum of 3 parts:

    - The drop-off section, which must be at least 1.5 feet tall.

    - A "hill" that the ball must pass over, which must be at least 8 inches tall.

    - The end section, where the ball should come to a stop.

65. MR AND MRS WRIGHT

Participants will close their eyes and listen to a story. Whenever they hear the words "left" or "right," they will turn in that direction.

Time required: 10 minutes.

Purpose: Enhance collaboration through goals and objectives clarity.

Number of participants: 8 to 50.

Space required: Small to large.

Preparation: None.

Conduct:

1. Find a spacious area where participants can comfortably turn their bodies around while staying in the same spot.

2. Have everyone stand up and face the front.

3. You will tell a story, and each time they hear the word 'right', they should turn their body 90° to the right.

4. When they hear 'left', they should turn 90° to their left.

5. They will do this activity with their eyes closed, and one hand covering their eyes.

6. Let them know that they can stop the activity if they feel uncomfortable.

7. After the story ends, tell the participants to open their eyes and stay looking in the same direction they were facing before. It's always funny when they see that some people are facing each of the four directions.

Story:

One evening they were baking cookies. Mrs. WRIGHT called from the kitchen, "Oh, no, there is no flour LEFT! You will need to go RIGHT out to the store."

"I can't believe you forgot to check the pantry," grumbled MR. WRIGHT. "You never get anything RIGHT!"

"Don't be difficult, dear," replied Mrs. WRIGHT. "It will only take twenty minutes if you come RIGHT back. Go to Fifty-first, turn LEFT at the stop sign. Then go to Sixty-first Street and turn RIGHT, and there it will be on your LEFT," declared Mrs. WRIGHT as her husband LEFT the house.

Mr. WRIGHT found the store and asked the clerk where he could find the flour. The clerk pointed and said, "Go to Aisle four and turn RIGHT. The flour will be on your LEFT."

Mr. WRIGHT made his purchase and walked RIGHT out the door. He turned LEFT, but he couldn't remember where he had LEFT his car.

Suddenly he remembered that he had driven Mrs. WRIGHT'S car and that his car was in the driveway at home RIGHT where he had LEFT it. He finally found the RIGHT car and put his purchase RIGHT inside. Eventually, a tired Mr. WRIGHT found his way home.

Mrs. WRIGHT had been waiting impatiently. "I thought you would be RIGHT back," she said. "I LEFT all the cookie ingredients on the kitchen counter, and the cat got into the milk. You'll just have to go RIGHT out again."

Mr. WRIGHT sighed. He had no energy LEFT. "I am going RIGHT to bed," he said. "Anyway, I need to go on a diet, so I might as well start RIGHT now. Isn't that RIGHT, dear?"

COMMUNICATION

66. STAND SIT 🖰

Every participant is given multiple numbers, and whenever their number is mentioned in the story, they must stand up.

Purpose: Encourage focused attention while listening.

Time required: 10 minutes.

Number of participants: 2 per group.

Space required: Small.

Preparation: Prepare two stories that involve lots of numbers.

Conduct:

1. Pair up the participant, with one person playing and the other refereeing.

2. Give each player 4 numbers to remember. All players should be given the same set of numbers.

3. Tell a story that involves numerous numbers.

4. Whenever the designated numbers are mentioned in the story, the players must stand up.

5. The referee will keep track of any instances where the players stood up incorrectly.

6. For the next round, have the players and referee switch roles.

7. Allocate a fresh set of numbers to the new players and narrate a new story.

67. SELL THIS ✍

Participants are given random objects found in the room and are then asked to deliver sales pitches to sell these items.

Purpose: Highlight the importance of asking questions to understand needs.

Time required: 20 minutes.

Number of participants: 2 to 5 per group.

Space required: Small.

Preparation: Flipchart papers and writing materials.

Conduct:

1. This activity is most effective with more than three groups.

2. Match the seller and buyer groups with each other, ensuring they avoid selling and buying from each other if possible.

3. Instruct the buying groups to randomly select an object from the room and pass it to their designated selling group. This object will be the one the seller needs to pitch to the buyer.

4. They will have 15 minutes to prepare a 5-minute sales pitch.

5. Avoid mentioning anything about asking questions to understand customers' needs to observe how teams utilize the 15-minute planning time.

6. Each group will take turns presenting their product pitch, and the buyer will assess the likelihood of purchasing the product.

68. SALT AND PEPPER

Everyone walk around asking yes or no questions to figure out what word is taped to their back. Then, they search for another person with a related word to make a pair of items.

Purpose: Practicing effective questioning techniques.

Time required: 10 minutes.

Number of participants: 10 to 50.

Space required: Medium to large.

Preparation:

- Create a list of item pairs, like salt and pepper, lock and key, Mickey and Minnie Mouse, and others.

- Write each item on its own piece of paper.

- Make enough pairs of items so that each participant gets one piece of paper. Repeat the pairs as needed.

- Get tape or enough cloth pegs ready to attach a piece of paper to each participant.

Conduct:

1. Attach one piece of paper to the back of each person, making sure they cannot see what's written on it.

2. Once everyone has received their assigned paper, they should walk around and ask only yes or no questions to discover the word taped to their back.

3. After figuring out the word, they need to find the person who has the matching word taped to them.

69. PAPER CUP PYRAMID

Participants guide their blindfolded teammates to build a paper cup pyramid.

Purpose: Practice giving clear instructions and practicing attentive listening.

Time required: 20 minutes.

Number of participants: 4 to 8 per group.

Space required: Medium to large.

Preparation:

- Blindfold for each participant.

- Table for teams to construct the pyramid, and place 30 stacked plastic cups on each table.

- Mark a starting line about 8 yards away from the table.

Conduct:

1. Divide the participants into 2 or more groups.

2. The objective of this activity is to construct a paper cup pyramid by stacking the paper cups on top of each other.

3. Each team can decide on the design they want to use for their pyramid.

4. Within each team, form sub-pairs of participants, where one person will be blindfolded, and the other will provide instructions.

5. One pair at a time will walk towards the table from the starting line. The blindfolded member will be guided by their partner during this process.

6. The rest of the team members will remain behind the starting line.

7. The blindfolded member, assisted by their partner, will begin the pyramid-building process by stacking two cups. Afterwards, they will return to the starting line.

8. Throughout the activity, the guiding partner is not allowed to physically touch the blindfolded partner or the cups.

9. If the pyramid collapses, the team will have to start from scratch.

10. All pairs will take turns building the pyramid, adding two cups at a time, in a rotational manner.

11. The pairs may switch roles during the activity but must remain with their original partner.

12. The team that builds the tallest pyramid wins.

70. CHARADES 🖱

A classic game that involves acting out words or phrases without speaking for others to guess.

Purpose: Emphasize the impact of nonverbal communication.

Time required: 15 minutes.

Number of participants: 10 to 25.

Space required: Medium to large.

Preparation: A set of words to act out.

Conduct:

1. Split the participants into two or three teams.

2. The teams will take turns playing.

3. Each team will choose one person to act while the rest of the team guesses.

4. The actor will act out the word or phrase without speaking.

5. After the round, it's the other team's turn to act out and guess.

6. If teams are playing multiple rounds, swap the actors.

71. PAPER TEARING ✄

Participants will receive instructions to tear a piece of paper while closing their eyes.

Purpose: Demonstrate how individuals understand messages in various ways.

Time required: 5 minutes.

Number of participants: 5 to 10.

Space required: Small.

Preparation: Paper for each person.

Conduct:

1. Give one paper to each person.

2. With their eyes closed, they will follow a set of instructions to tear the paper.

3. They must not ask any questions.

4. Give the following instructions one step at a time.

    -   Fold the paper in half.

    -   Tear off the upper right-hand corner.

    -   Fold the paper in half again.

    -   Tear off the lower right-hand corner.

    -   Fold the paper in half.

    -   Tear off the upper left-hand corner.

    -   Tear off the lower left-hand corner.

    -   Open your eyes, unfold your paper, and compare it with the others.

72. BUILDING BLOCKS

Participants communicate a design for a Lego model to their team mates to replicate the exact same design.

Purpose: Promote effective group communication.

Time required: 20 minutes.

Number of participants: 2 to 4 per group.

Space required: Medium to large.

Preparation:

- A space where participant can be hidden from each other.

- Lego models for each team and sufficient Lego bricks to recreate the model.

- Writing materials as needed.

- Ensure that participants are comfortable using their mobile phones for the activity.

Conduct:

1. Explain the activity to the groups and allow them ample time to work out their communication method.

2. The team will be split into two subgroups – A and B. A will receive a Lego model, while B will receive loose Lego bricks. The task is for the group with the loose bricks to recreate an exact replica of the Lego model.

3. Move subgroup A to a separate space where they are hidden from subgroup B.

4. Show the Lego model to subgroup A.

5. Provide subgroup B with the loose Lego bricks.

6. The subgroups can only communicate through verbal conversations using mobile phones.

73. WHAT IS THIS

Participants pass an object from one person to another while following a question-and-answer pattern.

Purpose: Emphasize the significance of effective and cohesive group communication.

Time required: 10 minutes.

Number of participants: 6 to 8 per group.

Space required: Small to medium.

Preparation: 2 random objects that are easy to handle, such as markers and tennis balls.

Conduct:

1. Assemble the participants in a circle and designate one person (referred to as A) in the group to initiate the activity.

2. Hand person A an object, in this case, a marker, which will be referred to as 'Ding' throughout the activity.

3. The team will create a pattern of passing the object and communication as follows:

   - Ding is passed to the next person in the circle.

   - The receiver then asks the passer, "What is this?"

   - The question is then relayed back through all the participants who have received the Ding, moving back to A in the sequence. - A will always respond to the question by saying, "This is a Ding.", and the answer will be relayed to the person who just received the object.

   - The pattern continues until the Ding travels through everyone in the group and is finally returned to A.

- If there are 8 people in the group, A will say "This is a ding" 7 times.

4. Once the group finishes passing 'Ding', hand another object, such as a tennis ball, to Person A. This second object will be referred to as 'Dong'.

5. The new objective is for the group to pass both 'Ding' and 'Dong' simultaneously in opposite directions, following the same pattern of passing and communication established earlier.

6. The person standing across from Person A in the circle will at some point be holding both 'Ding' and 'Dong'.

74. FIVE QUESTIONS 🖐

Participants are limited to asking only 5 questions to guess the identity of a famous personality.

Purpose: Practice effective questioning techniques.

Time required: 10 minutes.

Number of participants: 10 to 25.

Space required: Medium to large.

Preparation: Write the names of famous personalities on separate pieces of name tags and put them in a bag. Repeat names if needed.

Conduct:

1. Gather the group in a circle.

2. Participants will take turns drawing a name from the bag and attaching it to the back of the person on their right, without revealing the name to that person.

3. The name should be facing outward so that others can see it.

4. When you say "go," participants will individually meet 5 different people, one at a time, and ask each person a single question to find out the name on their back.

5. After asking the 5 questions, they should return to the circle.

6. Once everyone is back in the circle, each participant will take to guess the name of the person attached to their back.

75. DESCRIBE AND GUESS 🎙

The goal of this exercise is to explain a word to others without using the word itself.

Purpose: Practice speaking clearly with agility.

Time required: 15 minutes.

Number of participants: 8 to 15

Space required: Small.

Preparation:

- Prepare a list of words for the participants to describe or use an online word generator.
- If necessary, create a list of banned words for each participant, that they cannot use while describing the given word.

Conduct:

1. Each person has 60 seconds to describe a word, without saying the actual word, for the others to guess.

2. To ensure a meaningful and engaging activity, the person describing the word should avoid simply providing a list of substitute words, in addition to the banned words, while explaining the term.

76. BROKEN TELEPHONE

The goal is to see how a message changes as it is passed from one person to another, often resulting in amusing and unexpected outcomes.

Purpose: Encourage speaking directly to the source for clearer communication.

Time required: 5 minutes.

Number of participants: 8 to 10 per group.

Space required: Small to medium.

Preparation: A tricky tongue twister for the message, such as "Any noise annoys an oyster but a noisy noise annoys an oyster more"

Conduct:

1. Arrange the group in a line or a circle. This will be the order in which the message is passed from one person to the next.

2. Whisper the message to the first person quietly so that others can't hear.

3. Each participant, in turn, will whisper the message they heard to the person next to them.

4. They can't repeat the message; they can only say it once.

77. DRAW ON MY BACK

In this variation of the game "Broken Telephone", participants try to convey an image by drawing on each other's backs.

Purpose: Show how individual understanding of messages affects group communication.

Time required: 10 minutes.

Number of participants: 5 to 8 per group.

Space required: Small to medium.

Preparation: Writing materials and either tape or clothes pegs to attach the paper to the back of the participants.

Conduct:

1. Arrange the participants in a line, standing one behind the other.

2. The last person in the line will face a wall with a blank piece of paper stuck on it.

3. Everyone, except the first person, will attach a piece of paper to their back.

4. The first person will draw an image, one stroke at a time, on the back of the second person.

5. The second person will do the same on the back of the third person, and so on down the line.

6. Finally, the last person will replicate the drawing on the paper that is stuck on the wall.

7. If there are concerns about marker smudges on the clothes, then everyone can draw using their fingers on the back, except the last person who still needs to draw the image out.

78. THE DESTINATION ⬙

Participants create a list of items for a road trip. However, they later revise the list once they are informed about the destination.

Purpose: Highlight the importance of sharing goals and objectives early in communication.

Time required: 10 minutes.

Number of participants: 4 to 5 per group.

Space required: Small.

Preparation: Writing materials.

Conduct:

1. The group has 5 minutes to discuss and make a list of the things they need for a road trip.

2. Begin the activity right away, without waiting for any questions from them.

3. In the next round, give the group a destination and ask them to revise their list accordingly.

4. Participants will notice a difference between planning when they have a specific destination in mind and when they don't.

79. MINEFIELD

Participants lead their blindfolded teammates through a minefield to gather objects.

Purpose: Practice providing clear directions and active listening.

Time required: 15 minutes.

Number of participants: 5 to 8 per group.

Space required: Medium to large.

Preparation:

- Blindfold for each participant.
- Designate a starting line and arrange 20 green and 20 red plastic cups, placed face down, approximately 5 yards away from the starting line.

Conduct:

1. Divide the participants into 2 or more groups.
2. The objective of this activity is to gather the green cups without making any contact with the red ones.
3. One person at a time will enter the minefield blindfolded to retrieve the cups.
4. The remaining team members will stay behind the line and provide instructions.
5. If the person collecting the cup accidentally touches a red cup, they must return to the starting line and begin again.
6. Each person is allowed to collect only one cup at a time.
7. All team members will take turns in collecting the cups in a rotational manner.
8. The team that collects the most cups in 5 minutes wins.

80. BACK-TO-BACK ✆

Seated with their backs against each other, one person will describe a picture for another person to draw.

Purpose: Demonstrate how visual cues impact communication.

Time required: 10 minutes.

Number of participants: 2 per group.

Space required: Small to medium.

Preparation:

- A set of pictures and writing materials for each pair.
- If needed, provide a clipboard for the person who will be doing the drawing.

Conduct:

1. Pair up the participants.

2. Space out the groups to reduce cross talk, as it can become noisy during the activity.

3. Participants will sit back-to-back, and one person will describe a picture for another person to draw.

4. To increase the challenge, have a rule that the person drawing can't ask questions.

CREATIVITY

81. PAPER PLANE

Participants are tasked to make a paper airplane, but there's a twist that challenges their usual idea of what a paper plane should look like.

Purpose: Questioning assumptions and recognizing factors that limit creativity.

Time required: 10 minutes.

Number of participants: 1 to 2 per group.

Space required: Small to medium.

Preparation: A4 Paper.

Conduct:

1. Give each group a piece of paper.

2. Allow them 5 minutes to create a paper plane (avoid using the word 'fold').

3. Gather everyone at the starting line and have them all throw their planes at the same time.

4. The plane that flies the farthest will be the winner.

5. After all the planes have landed, inform them that it's your turn now.

6. Take a piece of paper and crumple it into the shape of a golf ball. This will be your "plane."

7. Toss your paper ball (plane), which will likely fly farther than most, if not all, of the other planes.

8. Some participants may object, questioning the design of your "plane."

9. Respond by asking why you should conform to the standard design.

82. PAPER TOWER

The goal of this activity is to construct the tallest tower using just a single piece of paper.

Purpose: Practice creative resource utilization.

Time required: 15 minutes.

Number of participants: 1 to 3 per group.

Space required: Small.

Preparation:

- Each group will need one A4 size paper, a pair of scissors, and 1 yard of sticky tape.

- Tables for groups to build the tower.

Conduct:

1. Hand out the materials to the group.

2. The task is to construct the tallest free-standing paper tower using only one piece of paper and the supplied sticky tape.

3. The group with the tallest tower wins.

83. THE EXPERTS

Two people volunteer as experts on a fun topic and answer questions from the audience.

Purpose: Encourage spontaneity in the creative process.

Time required: 15 minutes.

Number of participants: 8 to 25.

Space required: Small.

Preparation: Prepare an amusing topic, like "Shampoo and Conditioner for Lions."

Conduct:

1. Ask for two volunteers who are quick thinkers and invite them to come up to the front of the class.

2. Introduce them as Dr. (Name) and Prof. (Name), experts in the field of Lion Shampoo and Conditioner. They are here to answer any questions from the audience about their expertise.

3. Begin the activity and moderate the Q&A session.

84. PAPERCLIP 🖱

Participants are required to come up with as many ideas as they can for using paper clips.

Purpose: Practice brainstorming without judgment.

Time required: 10 minutes.

Number of participants: 1 to 3 per group.

Space required: Small.

Preparation:

- Writing materials.

- Optional: Paper clips for participants to play with.

Conduct:

1. Hand out writing materials and paper clips to the participants.

2. The task is to brainstorm various ways to use paper clips within a 5-minute time frame and record these ideas on the provided paper.

3. The team with the most creative answers will win.

85. ONCE UPON A TIME 🖰

Participants collaborate as a group to construct a story, taking turns to contribute three words at a time.

Purpose: Practice spontaneity in the creative process.

Time required: 5 minutes.

Number of participants: 10 to 25.

Space required: Small.

Preparation: None.

Conduct:

1. Arrange participants in a manner where everyone is clear about who goes next.

2. The first person will start the story with "Once upon a time…"

3. The next person will continue the story with only three words.

4. This pattern will continue until it's the last person's turn who will end the story with "… and that is why you need to eat your vegetables."

5. For smaller groups, consider continuing the story for a few rounds.

86. HANDSHAKE CHALLENGE

Participants work together in teams to come up with different special handshakes.

Purpose: Stimulate creative thinking.

Time required: 10 minutes.

Number of participants: 10 to 50.

Space required: Small to large.

Preparation: None.

Conduct:

1. Pair up the participants.

2. Their task is to create a unique handshake.

3. Encourage them to add sound effects.

4. Next, ask participants to form groups of threes with new partners.

5. They should invent a new handshake involving three people.

6. Continue the activity by making the group bigger.

7. Consider rewarding the most creative handshake teams to encourage participation.

87. BRAIN WRITING

This is a group brainstorming exercise where participants build upon each other's ideas to come up with creative solutions. This activity can also be applied to address real-life issues.

Purpose: Explore the benefits of idea synergy.

Time required: 15 minutes.

Number of participants: 8 to 15.

Space required: Small.

Preparation:

- Writing materials and ideally, a round table.

- A quirky question that begins with "how", for example, "How to encourage skydiving in the company?"

Conduct:

1. Hand out writing materials to each person.

2. Everyone writes the question at the top of their paper without adding their names.

3. Write one solution to the question and label it number "1."

4. Then, place their papers in the middle of the table and randomly select someone else's paper.

5. Add a new idea by building on the first one and label it "2." They must not repeat any solution they have provided.

6. The process continues until everyone has contributed to all the papers.

7. Everyone retrieves their paper and chooses the most effective solution from the compiled list.

8. Most of the time, participants tend to select someone else's idea as the most effective rather than their own.

88. NINE DOTS 🖱

The task is to connect all of the dots using four lines without lifting the pen.

Purpose: Promote thinking outside the box.

Time required: 5 minutes.

Number of participants: 1 to 2 per group.

Space required: Small.

Preparation:

- Make copies of this puzzle for each group or display it on a screen.

- Writing materials

Conduct:

1. Distribute the puzzle and writing materials.

2. The challenge is to connect all the dots using four lines without lifting the pen.

3. Teams that figure out the solution should keep it to themselves, so everyone has a chance to solve the puzzle.

Puzzle and Solution:

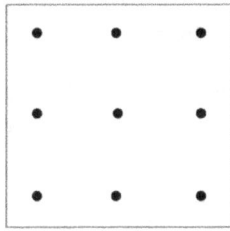 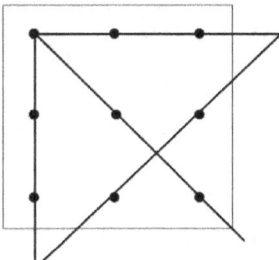

89. THREE CHANGES

Participants will play against their partners and make three changes to their appearance. The first person to spot all three changes will be the winner. The focus of this activity is what occurs after the game when participants revert the changes they made to their appearances without any prompting.

Purpose: Demonstrates the natural tendency to resist change.

Time required: 5 minutes.

Number of participants: 1 to 2 per group.

Space required: Small.

Preparation: None.

Conduct:

1. Pair up the participants.

2. They can play the game while standing or seated.

3. Participants should quickly scan each other's appearance from head to toe for 5 seconds.

4. When you say "go," they will turn around with their backs facing their partners and make three quick changes to their appearance.

5. When you say "go" again, they will turn back to face each other.

6. The first person to spot all three changes wins.

7. Afterward, facilitate some interaction by asking the group to share some hard-to-spot or interesting changes they noticed.

8. During the interaction, most, if not all, of the participants will undo the changes and revert to their original appearance.

9. Ask them why they do that even though you did not tell them to do so.

10. You will hear responses such as "it's more comfortable" and "it feels natural to undo the changes."

90. PRESENTATION ROULETTE 🖱

Participants are asked to give an impromptu presentation to a live audience on a new topic, without any prior preparation.

Purpose: Foster the ability to be comfortable with ambiguity and uncertainty.

Time required: 20 minutes.

Number of participants: 1 to 4 per group.

Space required: Small.

Preparation: Prepare presentation slides on different topics.

Conduct:

1. Ask a group to come to the front.

2. Every group will be given a random topic right before their presentation.

3. The presentation begins as soon as the introduction slide is shown.

4. Split the slides if there are multiple participants in a group.

PROBLEM-SOLVING

91. BALL DROP

The goal of this activity is to create a device that can catch a golf ball when it is dropped from a height.

Purpose: Practice problem framing and using available resources creatively to find solutions.

Time required: 20 minutes.

Number of participants: 2 to 4 per group.

Space required: Small to medium.

Preparation: 1 golf ball, 20 plastic straws and 1 yard of sticky tape for each group.

Conduct:

1. The objective is to create a device capable of catching a golf ball dropped from a height of 2 yards.

2. Use only the materials provided.

3. The device must be able to hold the golf ball securely when it catches it for the attempt to be considered a success.

4. Every team will choose a member to stand on a chair and drop the ball.

92. THREE JUGS PUZZLE ⌐⊖

The task is to measure 6 oz. of water using three different containers with varying volumes.

Purpose: Promote systemic thinking.

Time required: 20 minutes.

Number of participants: 1 to 3 per group.

Space required: Small to medium.

Preparation:

- Prepare three containers with volumes of 12 oz., 8 oz., and 5 oz., respectively.

- The containers must not have any volume markings.

- Fill the 12 oz. container to the top with either water or marbles, depending on what is more practical.

- If it's not possible to do this physically, conduct the activity as a puzzle on paper.

Conduct:

1. Distribute the containers or puzzle to each group.

2. The objective is to measure precisely 6 oz of water using only the three containers.

Solution:

	12 oz.	8 oz.	5 oz.
Start	12	0	0
Step 1	4	8	0
Step 2	4	3	5
Step 3	9	3	0
Step 4	9	0	3
Step 5	1	8	3
Step 6	1	6	5

93. STRAWS CONNECTION

The goal of this activity is to build a structure using 12 straws, following specific requirements.

Purpose: Practice logical thinking and experimentation.

Time required: 20 minutes.

Number of participants: 2 to 4 per group.

Space required: Small to medium.

Preparation:

- 12 non-bendable straws and some Blue Tack for each group.

Conduct:

1. Give each group 12 straws and some Blue Tack.

2. The task is to build a structure following these rules:

    - Use all 12 straws and as much Blue Tack as required.

    - All ends of each straw must be connected to another straw.

    - Keep parallel straws at least one straw length apart.

    - The structure must be able to stand on its own.

Solution:

Two four-sided pyramids that share the same square base. The object would be lying on its side.

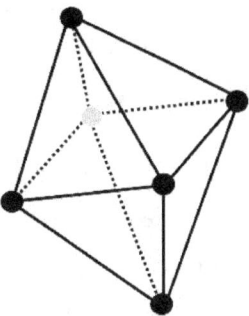

94. TRAFFIC JAM

The group is divided into two sides, and the goal of this activity is for each side to make their way to the opposite side by getting past the other team. To succeed, both sides need to work together to figure out the best approach and make the right moves.

Purpose: Promote systematic thinking and collaborative problem solving.

Time required: 15 minutes.

Number of participants: 8 to 12 per group.

Space required: Medium.

Preparation: Mark 9 spots on the floor in a line, assuming there will be 8 participants, with a gap of 3 feet between each spot.

Conduct:

1. Divide participants into two even groups (Side A and B).

2. Have both groups form vertical lines, with Side A facing Side B, and Side B facing Side A.

3. Everyone should stand on a spot, leaving an empty spot in the center to separate the two sides.

4. The task is to get Side A participants to Side B and Side B participants to Side A, with all members facing forward.

5. The starting order is: A B C D (empty spot) 1 2 3 4.

6. The ending order should be: 1 2 3 4 (empty spot) A B C D.

7. Throughout the activity, there will always be one spot left unoccupied, allowing team members to move and achieve the goal of the game.

8. Rules are as follows:

- No moving backwards.

- A person can only move forward to an empty space.

- A person cannot "jump over" someone from their side.

- One person from Side A or B is allowed to make a move at any given moment.

- One spot per person, no sharing.

- Rule violation requires a restart.

Solution:

Start	A>	B>	C>	D>		<1	<2	<3	<4
1	A>	B>	C>		D>	<1	<2	<3	<4
2	A>	B>	C>	<1	D>		<2	<3	<4
3	A>	B>	C>	<1	D>	<2		<3	<4
4	A>	B>	C>	<1		<2	D>	<3	<4
5	A>	B>		<1	C>	<2	D>	<3	<4
6	A>		B>	<1	C>	<2	D>	<3	<4
7	A>	<1	B>		C>	<2	D>	<3	<4
8	A>	<1	B>	<2	C>		D>	<3	<4
9	A>	<1	B>	<2	C>	<3	D>		<4
10	A>	<1	B>	<2	C>	<3	D>	<4	
11	A>	<1	B>	<2	C>	<3		<4	D>
12	A>	<1	B>	<2		<3	C>	<4	D>
13	A>	<1		<2	B>	<3	C>	<4	D>
14		<1	A>	<2	B>	<3	C>	<4	D>
15	<1		A>	<2	B>	<3	C>	<4	D>

16	<1	*<2*	A>		B>	<3	C>	<4	D>
17	<1	<2	A>	*<3*	B>		C>	<4	D>
18	<1	<2	A>	<3	B>	*<4*	C>		D>
19	<1	<2	A>	<3	B>	<4		*C>*	D>
20	<1	<2	A>	<3		<4	*B>*	C>	D>
21	<1	<2		<3	*A>*	<4	B>	C>	D>
22	<1	<2	*<3*		A>	<4	B>	C>	D>
23	<1	<2	<3	*<4*	A>		B>	C>	D>
24	<1	<2	<3	<4		*A>*	B>	C>	D>

95. WARP SPEED

The group is tasked to establish a pattern of throwing a ball and then find ways to improve the efficiency of the patterns.

Purpose: Encourage continuous improvement.

Time required: 30 minutes.

Number of participants: 10 to 25 per group.

Space required: Medium to large.

Preparation: 1 tennis ball.

Conduct:

1. Gather the group in a circle.

2. Pass the tennis ball to a volunteer, who will be the first person to pass the ball and the last person to receive it.

3. Instruct the volunteer to pass the ball to someone who is not standing directly beside them.

4. The receiver then passes the ball to another person, who will do the same to create a pattern of passing and receiving.

5. When the ball drops, the team will need to start over.

6. Everyone should receive and pass the ball only once.

7. Ask the group to repeat the pattern and you will time their attempt.

8. After each attempt, challenge them to try to improve their timing.

9. When participants ask for clarification on the rules, inform them that the only rule they need to follow is to throw and receive the ball from the same person.

96. ROUND AND ROUND

Participants must find the fastest way to pass a set of balloons.

Purpose: Encourage thorough understanding of the issue before taking any action.

Time required: 15 minutes.

Number of participants: 8 to 25.

Space required: Medium to large.

Preparation: 1 balloon for each participant.

Conduct:

1. Arrange the group in a circle.

2. Give each participant a balloon and instruct them to inflate it to the size of a basketball.

3. The task is to pass the balloons and have everyone retrieve their balloon as quickly as possible.

4. Balloons can only be passed to the person on their right.

5. The group must maintain a circular formation, and participants cannot change their positions.

6. Task will restart if any balloon falls to the ground.

7. Time each attempt and encourage the group to improve their timing.

8. After several attempts, inform them that the best teams can complete the task in under 3 seconds.

9. Challenge the group to meet the benchmark timing.

10. Reveal the solution: After the first pass, everyone should turn outward and face away from the center of the circle, then pass the balloon to the right, back to its owner.

97. FIND THE CHAIR

While blindfolded, the participants must move around a group of chairs to locate the correct one.

Purpose: Practice breaking down complex issues into smaller, manageable components.

Time required: 20 minutes.

Number of participants: 5 to 10.

Space required: Medium to large.

Preparation:

- Spread out 15 to 20 identical chairs around a spacious area.

- There should be 9 feet spacing between each chair.

- 1 blindfold for each person.

Conduct:

1. Gather the team outside the arena and show them the chair they need to find to complete the activity.

2. The team's task is to find that chair within 10 minutes, and they must do so blindfolded.

3. During the journey, the team must locate 2 extra chairs to use as checkpoints.

4. The group should move together in a line, ensuring that each member always maintains body contact with at least one other person.

5. Finding the chairs will only be considered successful when the first person in the line touches them.

6. The person at the front of the line can be changed at any time, but the trainer must be aware of who the current front person is.

98. SPAGHETTI TOWER

Teams are provided with a few supplies to construct the tallest tower capable of holding a marshmallow.

Purpose: Encourage prototyping and testing to create effective solutions.

Time required: 15 minutes.

Number of participants: 2 to 3 per group.

Space required: Small to medium.

Preparation:

- 1 marshmallow, 30 spaghetti sticks, 1 scissors, and 1 yard of sticky tape for each team.
- Tables to build the tower on.

Conduct:

1. The goal of this activity is to construct the tallest tower using spaghetti, and the marshmallow must be positioned at the very top.

2. The tower should be able to stand on its own without any external support.

3. Use only the materials provided.

99. TOXIC WASTE

The goal is to design a system that can transfer toxic waste (candies/balls) into a biohazard disposal container (bucket).

Purpose: Promote experimentation and collaborative problem solving.

Time required: 20 minutes.

Number of participants: 4 to 7 per group.

Space required: Medium to large.

Preparation:

- Mark a square with dimensions of 9 x 9 feet on the floor. Place a bucket right in the middle of the square.

- Gather the following materials for each team:

    o 1 container filled with candies or ping pong balls.

    o 1 metal bull ring that is wide enough for the container to slide through, leaving some space around it.

    o 1 large ball of twine that can be cut into different lengths.

    o 1 pair of scissors.

Conduct:

1. The objective is to use the given materials to create a system that can pour the toxic waste (candies/balls) into a biohazard disposal container (bucket).

2. The task will reset if any toxic waste spills on the ground.

3. No one, including any body parts of any person, is allowed to cross or hover inside the square. If this rule is violated, the task will restart.

ABOUT THE AUTHOR

Joey Ng

A dedicated training facilitator based in Singapore, Joey brings over 15 years of invaluable experience to his book "Purposeful Play: 99 Training Activities." As an internationally certified facilitator, Joey's passionate about fostering experiential learning through purposeful play. In his view, training should be more than just absorbing information; it should be an active and enjoyable journey that engages learners on a deeper level.

Alongside his wife Karmen, he shares the joy of parenting two wonderful children, actively involving them in the exciting activities found within the pages of this book (yes, the games are great for kids too!).

With a commitment to spreading effective training methodologies, Joey welcomes opportunities for train-the-trainer collaborations. For those seeking to connect, Joey can be reached at joeynzj@hotmail.com and is available on LinkedIn at https://www.linkedin.com/in/joeynzj.

ENGAGE AND ELEVATE TRAINING SERIES

Introducing the "Engage & Elevate Training Series" – a collection of books packed with innovative ideas, interactive activities, and practical strategies to transform mundane training sessions into vibrant learning experiences.

Whether you're a seasoned trainer or new to the field, the "Engage & Elevate Training Series" provides the tools and inspiration needed to create impactful and memorable training programs that drive success. Elevate your training sessions from ordinary to extraordinary with this essential resource for modern corporate learning.

Purposeful Play: 99 Interactive Training Activities: Games and exercises for engaging and effective learning.

Available on Amazon.

Dive into 'Purposeful Play: 99 Interactive Training Activities' and discover a treasure trove of handpicked games, icebreakers, and exercises. These activities aren't just any games – they're carefully chosen to add a spark of energy and meaning to your training sessions.

Imagine breaking down walls between participants, sparking meaningful conversations, and boosting valuable skills. That's exactly what these activities are designed to do. Drawing from the author's own experiences, this collection is like a secret recipe for creating genuine connections and memorable learning moments. Whether you want to supercharge teamwork, ignite creativity, or give your group a boost of energy, each activity is a powerful tool.

As a trainer, you hold the key to transforming learning into an unforgettable adventure. With these activities at your fingertips, you can create learning experiences that are not only effective but also immensely enjoyable. Get ready to infuse your sessions with curiosity, camaraderie, and connection – one purposeful play at a time!"

Beyond Boredom: Elevating Engagement in Corporate Training "Beyond Boredom: Ideas for engaging and effective learning.

Available on Amazon.

Elevating Engagement in Corporate Training" offers a refreshing perspective on shaking up traditional training methods that often leave participants uninspired. In a world filled with distractions and shrinking attention spans, the old "sit-and-listen" approach falls short. The book challenges trainers to rethink their strategies and inject life into their sessions to capture genuine interest and enthusiasm from modern learners.

Contrary to popular belief, being an engaging trainer isn't solely about charisma or entertaining antics. It's about intentional design and delivery, ensuring every aspect of the training serves a purpose and encourages meaningful participation. Regardless of personality type, trainers can create impactful learning experiences that resonate with their audience.

While humor and interactive activities are valuable tools, true engagement requires thoughtful planning and structure. From the flow of the session to the content delivery, every element should contribute to a dynamic and enriching learning environment. "Beyond Boredom" guides trainers through the process of creating engaging training sessions that leave a lasting impact on learners.